A slice of Life

Claudia Clark

$\mathbb{C}$lark

In loving memory of

Romano Barbieri

1938-2001

Father and daughters 1979

THANKS GO TO

My husband Edward and my family for their patience reading hundreds of my poems and supporting my work, to Kate Milloy and AIA, to Michael Dalby and MRD, to Alec Philpott for his photography and website design and to my friends for their ideas and experiences which helped to shape the book.

And to **you**, for buying my book and supporting Cancer Research UK and the Duchess of Kent House Trust.

Thank you.

Claudia

Introduction

ABOUT THE AUTHOR

A Slice of Life is Claudia Clark's first book. She was born in 1975 in Wokingham, Berkshire and now lives in St. Margaret's in Middlesex. The book is inspired by a love of poetry and fuelled by the loss of her father to cancer in 2001.

WHY HAVE I WRITTEN A SLICE OF LIFE?

Cancer used to be the word that no one dared utter, that made us shrink and feel uncomfortable, a conversation stopper at any table. But times are changing, we are talking about it, and the more we learn to talk about our experiences of cancer, the better.

WHAT CAN YOU DO?

Talking, like writing poetry, can be liberating. Being able to talk about cancer requires us to find someone who can listen without trying to find an answer or solution; someone who can just sit and hold our hand.

My hope is that the section of the book on 'Friends and Family' will provide an insight into the unique emotions cancer stirs, and that you can be the listener when someone needs you.

WHAT ABOUT THE PROCEEDS OF THE BOOK?

The proceeds from the sale of this book will be split between Cancer Research UK and The Duchess of Kent House Trust in Reading.

Enhancing the quality of life for patients

Cancer Research UK has a mission to conquer cancer through world-class research. Cancer Research UK is now the largest volunteer-supported cancer research organisation in the world, with a team of 3,000 scientists.

Cancer Research UK aims to:

- cure cancer patients faster
- cut numbers of people getting cancer
- bring better treatments to cancer patients
- train more cancer doctors, nurses and scientists for research
- be the authoritative source of information on cancer
- maximise resources available for cancer research

Cancer research is providing you and I, and our friends and families with the chance to live without, with and beyond cancer.

Contents

Friends and family

Diagnosis *8*
Yesterday *9*
Remission *10*
Beyond *11*
Hand in Hand *12*
Carnival *13*
Moment *14*
Dreaming *15*

NATURE AND NURTURE

Gatherer *18*
Reading on the Underground *19*
Advice *20*

Sandpits and Star Wars

Fairies can *36*
Play *37*
The Station *38*
Did you? *39*
Babe *40*
Swell *41*
0 - 26 years *42*
Another place *43*

Learning and Loving

Side *22*
A rest in your music *23*
Liberation *24*
Called *25*
Holiday *26*
...More Fish *27*
Sensation of love *28*
Washing-up *29*
Thai *30*
The leather handbag *31*
Written in the stars *32*
Holding hands *33*

Headlines and History

Q of ❤ *46*
09.11 *47*
Waiting *48*
Elizabeth *49*
Right on *50*
Angolan childhood *51*

Tickets and Footprints

Florence *54*
Rome *55*
Two Worlds *56*
A 21st century tale *57*
Mama *58*
Venice *59*

Puzzles and Pictures

Poetry *61*

Friends and family

What cancer snatches away from our lives with one
hand, it can give back with another. It can alter our
relationships and perspectives forever. Despite its
devastating effects, cancer can give us the chance to
appreciate and to celebrate who we are and who we
love. It can bind us closer together than we ever knew
was possible.

Smile on.

Stand tall in the seated room,
Laugh loud in the silent gallery.
Strive on in driving rain,
Lean heavy on those around you.

Smile on.

Be how you always are,
Don't change now you are a statistic.
Talk openly to be liberated,
Lean heavy on those who care.

Smile on.

Give people the chance to see you,
Forget that they don't understand.
Look forward, they are behind you,
Lean heavy on those who love you.

Smile on.

You are not alone.
Lean heavy.

Diagnosis

We would have cherished the candyfloss,
Melting like pink butter on our tongues,

Would have danced, sung loud and bold,
Would have smiled and laughed together,

Would have.

If we had known the fair would end,
The crowds abandon,
And the rain lash down merciless.

Yesterday

Remission

He lies above us.

She in the garden,
I in a poem,
Practicality is our poison.
Away from tight,
Tormenting minds.
We are swallowing hard.
Denying the floodwaters,
Which are brimming daily
To burst.
Voices quiver,

A moment.
Focus.
We recompose.
For it is not the time to weep.

yond

All voice is gone from my head
My soul is silenced,
Void of anguish to churn my stomach
Or crease my forehead.
Pain has gone, just peace remains,
I am drifting.

Letting my eyes transport you beyond the
Window pane, up into the clouds, tumbling
Flying, dancing to a million melodies
Trumpeting your song, buoyant and long.
To lie deep in cool grasses rippling like thin
Green knives, stroking your damp skin
Kind and long, wet and calm around you.
To dive weightless in the pools, light gone and
Darkness cradling you in its silence
Bursting the bubbles of your breath,
as you transcend

Towards the light.

They are waiting for you beyond the pane, soon enough
In your head will be the noise that is you.

Hand in Hand

Take my hand and let us wander,
Deep into the thick
Forest of purple and white.
And lie silent on the dewy banks,
And tempt our toes at the cool river.
To look high at the serene sky blinking with a hundred eyes

And be together for a million moments.
Let us hold hands again, warm and calm and close.
Let us be together always in this picture,
We belong in this vision tonight and always.
I know I will always find you here,
Where we can wander hand in hand for eternity.

The wheels of life keep on turning
Unyielding and hard,
Carving and shaping the paths of our lives
Once full with such sweet chaos, then - suddenly empty,
and still.

As carnival road is desolate now in the aftermath of celebration
Save for the whisper of sweet wrappers twisting the pavements.
Vibrancy, sounds and energy dispersed.
All, but a memory of life hangs in the air.

For as darkness falls on the trodden ground
There is a silence I have never known.

You are gone.

Carnival

Moment

Don't wait
Until you stand at a grave side.

Hiding in the chaos, forgetting to phone,
Remembering not to write.

Too proud, stubborn, and strong,
It will be gone.

Snatched like the silky cobweb,
You forgot to admire

Crushed to nothing.
And you will stand at a rainy grave,

Grasping your dying roses, talking
To a ton of fresh turned soil.

Dreaming

You are there again,
Always smiling so warm
Normal and real.

You tempt me again,
To believe, to touch you
Normal and real.

Morning smacks again.
Reality bites so
Normal and real.

NATURE AND NURTURE

This is a short collection of poems about human nature. Despite society's diversity, hosting an array of ages, cultures and outlooks some mannerisms still remain the same.

Gatherer

Box up the polished cutlery gleaming,
Lock the fragile china away in darkness tight.
Display with care the white stringed candle,
Save the expensive bath oil for another night.

Hide with caution the inherited opal ring,
Polish and place special shiny shoes away.
Dust the lava-lamp in the corner cold,
Save the French perfume for another day.

Don't crack the spine of the book you bought,
Stow away the rich truffles in their silky pack,
Leave the champagne bottle dusty on the rack,
Remember to renew the Morris Minor's off road tax.

Consider for a moment as you gather,
Save, box, and hide things you cherish.
Tomorrow is yet untold and we may be lost,
These trinkets we harbour may be left to perish.

Scratch and smear the mirrored cutlery daily,
Load the bath with bubbles to relax and clean,
Stain the china with tea or chip with washing,
And melt the slender candle tall and lean.

Wear with joy Grandmother's only gem,
Light the lava to dance and tumble,
Splash with vigour sweet fragrance on your skin,
Wear and scuff the shiny shoes as you stumble.

Bend the pages of the book you love to read,
Launch the champagne cork to celebrate whatever,
Munch on forbidden truffles rich,
Fill up the Morris and drive just for pleasure.

Consider for a moment as you gather,
Save, box, and hide things you cherish.
Tomorrow is yet untold and we may be lost,
These trinkets we harbour may be left to perish.

Reading on the Underground

Erect in his pin stripes he peruses his long pink paper.
Eyes skirting the edges to glimpse his neighbour's third page.

Who's worn hands turn over another pert pair, bored he drifts to the
Lady opposite's paper plastered with a daily murder sensation,

She skips the pages, full of celebrity scandal
Glancing at the magazine held in loose hands opposite

By a fresh faced girl, calculating a banal multiple-choice.
Smug with her paperback, a women re-reads page 76 for the third time.

I am watching her from my poetry book as the man opposite studies me
Curious; I flicker my eyes; he retreats to his paper, scolded.

Text is always brighter on another page.

Advice

Go past the crumbling post office on the bend,
Beyond the school tightly fenced with railings,
Wind towards the old bench in the corner, worn.

Keep on, and soon across the horizon, emerging you will
See the cottages speckled on the hillside careless,
The river will be twisting beside you, bubbling gently.

Morning will be breaking, and you will hear
The thrush calling shrill and long across the sky.
The road will be twisting you into unknown bends, blind.

Once slight markings will disappear as the path narrows,
Suddenly an open landscape will reveal itself exposed, cold.
You will pass loose horses in the fields thundering.

They will gallop with you playful; racing, and chasing.
The afternoon will be upon you as the road rises over
The faint brow, and then down deep into a valley, wooded.

Soon the road will become vague, and rough,
You will bump on uneven ground, sore.
But then you will arrive, unexpected in the clearing.

Light will penetrate through the lofty trees
To a bright patch on dull ground, and you will see
The box glint in the sunlight.

What brought you here to this moment?
Maps and scribbled notes, and long narratives learnt?
Or just the voice in your head... Go past the crumbling

Learning and Loving

We all have elements of our lives that we would rather dust away with the cobwebs; hard experiences that have shaped who we are. Equally, we all have the bright, yellow warm aspects that make us smile, and help us grow.

Side

In your eyes I am home,
Lost somewhere, in deep crevasses of animation.
Or drifting contented in a story recounted,
And complete somehow in your silent hold,

Where the rise and fall of your chest sedates me,
And in the darkest moment I am still smiling
With you by my side.
In your eyes I am home.

A rest in your music

Moments of anger shall form and divide
Passions will ignite, and kindness hide.

Corner will be fought and cases heard,
Tongues to chastise so hard with words.

An aftermath like a tidal wave will unfold
With the ache of regret silent and cold.

Yet this sore heat is but a moment fleeting.
Sudden, unprecedented as a chance meeting.

It is more like the rest as music pounds,
A momentary pause to contrast the sounds.

For beyond the rest a crescendo will rise
With vigour and passion doubled in size.

And the moment of rest is a necessary clause,
To learn the beauty that surrounds its pause.

The audience of music won't hear the rest,
Only see the strong rhythm you together possess.

As your music plays on you will learn the rests
Will surrender to their moment; deny the contest.

Your melody growing will rise and fall, as it must
And the changes and rests will be cradled by trust.

Hand in hand as your worlds now beautifully collide.
Together you will be, in your music side by side.

LIBERATION

And so to uncertain silence
Light slumber, cold tea.

A wet November night pricks my skin,
Sultry clouds monopolise the sky.

His car wheels spin off on wet leaves,
I wander.

Willows whisper a conspiracy
To the west winds.

Water cascades my cheeks.

Called

Cold pillows.
A breeze dances over bare skin newly kissed.

Radio warns.
Wine glasses leak sideways on cream carpet.

Half empty cupboards
Look upon an empty picture frame

Boot mud trails towards the door.

The siren calls.

Holiday

On this, Our sweet Italian snapshot,
Of soft light and sublime touch.
I remembered you.
Like a fat finger,
On a perfect photograph
Dark, blurred and ridiculous.
Had I scissors I would have cut you out.
Save you taint this vision somehow.
And though I have almost cut you out,
You were there once.
The negative is in an old box somewhere in a dusty attic
With a thousand other dark memories.
Locked.

Teardrops dissolve in her gravy
As rain in dirty puddles.
She leans heavy on clean cutlery
Like crutches.

The family converse silently above her head
Mouthing and frowning,
Mother kindly rubs her sad shoulder,
They fumble on between the courses, cautious.

Granny sighs, carving her meat with intent,
'If I had my time again I would be a lesbian'
What priceless pearls she wears.
Grandad nonchalantly chases a pea around his plate.

...More Fish

Sensation of love

An unleashed tap, a runaway train,
A roaming spider, a dancing flame,
A falling box, a brakeless car,
A fraying jumper, liquid tar,
Melting ice-cream, the rising sun,
Morning bird song, a shot from a gun.

A pallid watercolour, a vivid oil,
The heights of laughter, the lows of toil,
A west wind's whisper, a trumpet crescendo,
Mirroring bodies, innocent innuendo,
Today, tomorrow, rest or flight,
Surrendering arms, insistence to fight.

The heart beats this intoxicant song
Reverent, pure, resounding and long,
A smile punctuates daily thought
Like a melody that leaves the body taught.
The heart races with scent or sound
And with touch or whisper home is found.

Washing-up

She smiles on through the washing-up suds.
The shallow ocean wrinkles her hands,
Like cruel old age creeping,
Paws blind; chasing sharp cutlery,
Mindful guides white crockery to safety.
A grater attacks her beneath spoilt waves.
Silent, she smiles on through the washing-up suds.

Thai

We drink our deep soup
Of lime and spice.

Eyes water from the heat.

A hundred heads nod and chatter
Amidst the soup, noodles and clatter.

The leather handbag

She forgot her file
That's why she went home,
She had been in a hurry
That's why she forgot.

It was by the stairs.
She was humming as she arrived
Gravel crunched underfoot, so

Did not register the unknown car
Did not question the mac on the chair
Did not wonder why music drifted.
It was by the stairs
The leather handbag.
The owner's laughter echoed.
She climbed the stairs

Knowing before its summit the spectacular view.
Sheets flying, clothes discarded and
'Anvil and Hammer' loud on the radio.

She forgot her file
That's why she went home.
She had been in a hurry
That's why she forgot.

Written in the stars

Written in the soft galaxy black
Faint with stars dissolving,
Growing and turning,
Was cast the lovers spell
A million years ago.

And it was pledged that
Against battle or human folly
Their love would prevail,
Seamless and timeless
For a million years.

And when the wind would
Thrash them careless, their
Bodies would cling in tight concave,
And when the sun caressed light their skin
They would dance beneath the rays.

And as the stars foretold
Their love would blaze
In spent time,
All those who saw them
Smiled knowing the spell

That they would be together
Always beneath the storm,
Sun or moon
Hand in hand for eternity,
For a million years.

In the silence of despair and
The crescendo of success
You will hold hands

In the heat of disparity,
And the tranquillity of rest
You will hold hands.

As time is spent and
The world evolves around
You will hold hands with

The ease of children care-free,
Touch of first love and
The tie of blood.

Together you are joined
To grow and ebb
Sharing heart and mind

Forever holding hands.

Holding hands

Sandpits and Star Wars

What do you recall from your childhood? Trumpton, The Wombles of Wimbledon and flower fairies, or sherbet dips and flying saucers... What are the secrets locked away in a child's imagination, how can we tap into them?

When we are fairies we can

Dance on white clouds,
Or sleep in a cobweb

Can dine on a water lily,
Or smell a daisy's perfume

Can sing the bird's song,
Or shop the seabed for hours.

We can swim in a teardrop,
Or hide in a matchbox.

We just can.

Outside she weaves daisy chains for white fairies,
Or mixes her finest coffee from the garden's darkest mud.

Inside she towers bright Lego, or moulds soft plasticine
Back to front in dad's old shirt she finger-paints a masterpiece.

Quiet on warm carpet she rolls marbles with a friend,
Or gallops the hill-side to Black Beauty on cassette.

With soft breezes she blows bubbles, like a drifting melody
To a land of sweet imagination.

She likes to lick the cake mixture bowl when you bake, but
Most of all she smiles when you stop at her café to sample her drinks,

She loves you to visit her busy town and run up the steepest tower,
When you hang her art in the playroom, or crooked on the fridge, she smiles.

You are her friend, her customer, her chief fairy, or her gallery curator.
You are an irreplaceable fragment of imagination.

The Station

I tight rope walk the yellow line,
The crocodiles will eat me if I slip.
They circle beneath beady eyed,
Hungry for school uniformed meat.

The space train arrives at last!
I jump on board.
It is 10 minutes to the Moon I heard,
but only 5 to Mars.

Dad is on his mobile to the Space Security
Officers in the Government.
He is getting instructions for our mission.
We are top secret agents, (only Mum knows)

'Eeeerrrrrhh, nnnnneeeeeeeeooooooooooweeeee.
We have lift off!' –
Slap.
Dad is not a spy like me.

I must be quiet on the train.

Did you?

Did you collect milk bottle tops,
Press, clean and save them
For some unknown good deed?

Did you sit glued to the box
Serious with sticky back plastic
Chopping at loo rolls and egg cartons?

Did you visit daily your proud washing-up bowl
Of wobbly frog spawn,
Anxious for the day they would graduate?

Did you make chicken soup, casserole and pies
From dried wood bark, served with the finest
Mud gravy, selling rose petal perfume?

Did you drag your feet to Church, reluctantly
Tuck in your shirt, speak when spoken to
And wash you hands before a meal?

Did you ask to watch the TV, eat your greens
Dread school report time and get grounded for
All kinds of innocence.

Did We forget the sweetness of growing up?

She swells like a soft rose bud
Growing and widening.
Before our eyes –
Yet, not before them.
Within the velvet walls
Whispers of a new life begin.
Anonymous hands and toes
Nuzzle the blissful warmth.
In the kind darkness an imagination is growing.

Babe

Swell

She holds him in loose arms with ease,
Wandering with soft waves drifting her thighs
Sunlight tickles the water, throwing it's diamonds
Carelessly, and she blinks behind sepia glasses.
Her touch is a known warmth on his bare skin,
He giggles as the sea tickles his toes.
With her he is home and the vast ocean is
Inconsequential, the heat from her warm breasts
Lulls him, and the noise of the beach is lost to sleep.

Age 0 - 26yrs

I bit you,
I scratched you,
I pulled your hair.

Told on you
Whined at you
Stomped and stared.

I copied you
Watched you
Mimicked and spied

Began to know you
Began to love you
At last began to try.

You advised me
And helped me
Listened and smiled.

Were never angry
But so calm
Soft and mild.

We began
As we grew
To laugh and confide

Much more than
Just siblings
Thrown side by side.

For sister you are
More special than
You see.

Despite all that
Biting, you are
A best friend to me.

Another place

'Where is daddy?'
'He has gone to another place.'
'Can I visit him?'
'No, not in the usual way."

'Close your eyes my love
Sink deep into the bedclothes warm
And drift - drift away.
And soon he will find you.

Together you can visit all kinds of places
You can fly in soft tumbling clouds,
You can swim in the ocean for hours
You can wonder deep jungles, hunting.

He will always be waiting for you
When you shut your eyes
Here you can talk and laugh
Run and play, and kiss.

Sleep my love and soon he will find you.'

Headlines and History

We are witnesses daily to all kinds of tragedy,
a multitude of harrowing events compete for
the front pages of the papers.

Q of

We cried aghast with confusion.
An icon erased like a misspelt word,
On a royal tableau.

Children unaware, men gulping,
Women sisterless.
A black tidal wave engulfed the globe.

And we swarmed desperate to glimpse,
To grasp, to have a moment.
Yet they stood dry eyed.

Pictures of a thousand low eyes
and soft words.

An age of innocence was lost in a camera flash.

09.11

Knives and planes. Obliterated towers collapse like Lego in a talcum powder Dust ball, they scramble, like children in a desperate hide and seek. 20,21,22 screaming, gasping, pushing in an asthmatic rush, hurtling themselves to some imaginary safety, worn briefcases sing with cellular

Phones a million messages never to be known, she is sobbing into a cold hand set of horror, you can see her soft face smiling at you in the darkness, the sea of moaning bodies envelops you, holds you for a moment in its swell, and the fireworks ignite overhead... 99, coming ready or not.

A slice of Life

Waiting

Planes circle like hawks.
We lie rigid,
Masks under our beds,
Petrol in the shed, hidden.
Full moon bulges out,
A silver bauble on a
Grey iced cake.
Shining in the cold skies
Somewhere in the swelling abyss
May be an answer,
Lingering on the breeze.
Or in a dark cupboard of
Some imagination.
Locked.
Soon the postman will deliver.

Elizabeth

Grey mourning on London Town.
Blackened commuters raise
Portraited papers.

Shops to close
Offices to pause
Flowers thrown

People mourn
A family pained
A page in history is turned.

Right on

We glide under dark bridges
Mossy and cool
Punctuated from bright light.

A hundred feet are pedalling
Metal frames
Over cobbled bridges.

Sleek trams nudge the blanket
Of visitors from their path
Like a babe hot with summer.

Strangers smile in abundance,
Their imaginations drift in
Smoke rings a moment

Amid the haze the street riot
Swells, and heaves like heavy breath,
A gunshot is lost in the chaos.

Angolan childhood

Flies buzz with intent
Around his wobbly head.
His brown hollow stomach
Bloated as a woman heavy with child
Shining like a bright chestnut made for play.
His life swings on a fragile rope, knotted tight.
His heart is drilled - soon to be smashed.
Time and rice, rice and time
Flies buzz with intent
Around his head,
Still.

Tickets and Footprints

We may wander carefree on the tourist traps we frequent, what might we be missing in our shot-gun visits? What rumbles beneath the surface of these sun tickled towns and cities?

A million foot steps are parading the marble floors,
To glimpse high ceilings, with low intentions.
Rustling maps and debating dinner
Cooing at candles and pledging an annual prayer.

Christ's statue another number on a camera reel
Of beach snaps and hilarities.
A well fenced alter is denied, attempting to preserve
What has already been lost in the onslaught of tourism.

Nothing stirs within these walls; a shell of architecture
Once swollen with Spirit, hostless is now barren and cold.

Florence

Rome

Once proud sun bleached walls.
Now faint pastel towers are
Discarded ruins redundant; as abandoned
Toys, on a nursery floor. Careless.

Inconsequential in a throbbing city
Whirls bleating traffic
And herding colourful tourists,
Who stumble on a million moments of history,

Hanging in the pauses of conversation.
A fleeting reference to a time before,
Too complex to know,
And timely to study.

We roam briefly, on this, another page to
The catalogue of stories to remark upon,
In smoky pub, spoilt Sunday lunch or
Acquaintance tit-bit, brief.

Rome is done.

A slice of Life

Two Worlds

What is the pulse of Africa
So fragmented;
Torn, sewn and bound
With dry reeds, and glazed with
Sweet candle light, or a faint
Lampala bleating.

Or dull and smoky, as a
Tin-can town, and all
Busy like ants with treasures.
And so bold in a litter filled
Haven teeming with hope and
Strong with resolve.

In the bush the light is
Slowly fading against a mottled sky,
In low cities the fire's cinders glow red
Fences are growing here like disease
Electric lines cage men from the animals,
Nothing separates men from themselves.

A 21st century tale

Sleepy city rife with paradox.
Matriarchy is meeting Man
In dimly lit corridors and
A conundrum rages.
Pretty girls with loaded rag dolls, meet
Handsome boys raising forlorn rifles.

Voices echo in a distant hallway,
Where once soft spoken ladies in white
Silk and cotton drifted a wooden dance
Floor, as he twisted her on and on...
Like a jewellery box doll in perpetual pirouette
Now dance is gone the box is silenced.

She marches cold corridors erect in her pinstripes.
Rehearsed in her banter of finance and forecasts.
Deadline and data the suckling dependents, bring fulfilment
In this world, so devoid of music.
He too wanders the corridors creased shirted with unpolished shoes
Ravenous for breakfast and heavy breathed with hurry.

The game is lost already.
They blink in black corridors alone.

Mama

She reigns, soft smiles and light hands
Territorial in her wake.
Patting her mosquito squatter against
Summer's indigestible heat.

Mrs Hamlet is cast
On a Sicilian rural stage,
Where overripe tomatoes tickle the senses
And the penned home grown await their fate.

His two women sit adjacent in the speckled shade like heavyweights.

He shelters behind dark shutters,
Treading the marble floor he should not sweep
Around the stove he should not know.
In soliloquy he is torn.

Across a dusty horizon a storm is swelling,
A temperate sky will be lost to a certain thunder.
A bell tolls.
The ring is anyone's.

Venice

From the dusty train stations we trot
Released at last from its heat
And all at once you are before us
Serene and splendid, like a great aunt
Patiently awaiting our annual visit.
And we are captured somehow into this pastel vision
Which twists before us, your choppy waters wide and kind
Enveloping us in this watery world.

St Marks casts a spell upon us and
A thousand others as the afternoon sun kisses the roof tops
Dancing abstract dramas on the well worn ground.
A smiling quartet sprinkling the air with sweet strings
And a million pigeons play court jester to their audiences.
The narrow back stages bustle with local fare
Carefully mastered crafts, stunning glassware tempting us
To masquerade a while in this theatrical city of beauty.

Puzzles and Pictures

Poetry. What is it all about? Poetry can be whatever
we want it to be, It can be a disciplined art form,
an expression of love, a therapy, a form of humour,
a political statement, a thought provoker or a story.

Above all, poetry is a puzzle for the reader to
piece together.

We lost the right corner one Christmas,
Three pieces gone,
an artist's signature
Swallowed by the dog,
Or snuffled by the Hoover.

A chance for some forgotten silence,
To ponder the pieces, and attempt blind
Reconstruction, grabbing at colours,
Forcing the wrong piece in a hole without

A nook or two crannies.
And the lid lost too.
So we fumble on between stewed tea,
Dry turkey sandwiches, and Only Fools and Horses.

Poetry

'Lean heavy'

'Sweet imagination'

'Long across the sky'

'When we are fairies'

'Text is always brighter on another page'

'Fences are growing here like disease'

'Wide and kind'